MW01128252

Help for the Caregiver

Facing the Challenges with
Understanding and Strength

Michael R. Emlet

New
Growth
Press
www.newgrowthpress.com

All Scripture quotations, unless otherwise indicated, are taken from the *Holy Bible,* New International Version®, NIV®. Copyright © 1973, 1978, 1984 by International Bible Society. Used by permission of Zondervan. All rights reserved.

New Growth Press, Greensboro, NC 27404
Copyright © 2008 by Christian Counseling & Educational Foundation. All rights reserved. Published 2008

Cover Design: The DesignWorks Group, Nate Salciccioli and Jeff Miller, www.thedesignworksgroup.com

Typesetting: Robin Black, www.blackbirdcreative.biz

ISBN-10: 1-934885-50-9
ISBN-13: 978-1-934885-50-5

Library of Congress Cataloging-in-Publication Data

Emlet, Michael R.
  Help for the caregiver / Michael R. Emlet.
     p. cm.
  Includes bibliographical references and index.
  ISBN 978-1-934885-50-5
  1. Caring—Religious aspects—Christianity. 2. Caregivers—Religious life. I. Title.
  BV4647.S9E45 2008
  259'.4—dc22
                                        2008011940
Printed in Canada
20 19 18 17 16 15 14 13   11 12 13 14 15

George is not the same man he used to be. A year ago he had a stroke that partially paralyzed him. Not only did the stroke affect George physically, it also affected his personality and behavior. Once a successful and competent, corporate attorney who faithfully served in his church, he now spends most of his day sitting in a chair. Most of the time he is passive and withdrawn, but he can also be impatient and demanding. Some days the littlest thing sets him off, and he explodes with rage or becomes tearful and clingy. Often his humor is coarse and sexually lewd. These are all new behaviors for George, and his family is struggling with how to respond. When they try to talk to him about his behavior, he is either oblivious or defensive.

His family is heartbroken, confused, discouraged, and angry. They want to have compassion for George's suffering, but they feel drained by his unrelenting neediness. They are grieving his change from a loving and humble husband and father to a man who doesn't seem to care much about them. And they have lots of questions. They are wondering how to understand the changes in George's personality, how to love and help the "new" George, and how to live with hope under the pressure of constant caregiving.

If you are a caregiver for someone who is chronically ill, you are probably asking the same kinds of questions. This booklet will give you a framework to guide you as you care for someone with ongoing physical and mental problems. Although the specifics of providing care for stroke victims, Alzheimer's sufferers, or those with bipolar disorder are very different, there are general principles you can apply to your situation that will help you to think biblically, act lovingly, and persevere even when you feel like throwing in your caregiving towel.

Everyone Is Made in God's Image

When we use a phrase like, "he's the spitting image of his father," we usually mean that the son displays the physical characteristics of his earthly father. He looks (and perhaps acts) like his dad. In a similar, but far more profound way, we resemble the God of the universe, both in his character and actions. You and the person you are caring for are created in the image of God (Genesis 1:26–28; Psalm 8:4–8).

God made us to reflect his image to the world. We don't do this perfectly because of sin and disease, but no matter what our disabilities, we never stop imaging God! George is no less an image bearer after the stroke than he was before the stroke. The person you are caring for also bears God's image.

The gospel is about renewing the true image of God through Jesus (Ephesians 4:24; Colossians 3:10). This process is not derailed by illness and disability. Instead, God uses these things to make us more like him. God promises he will complete the work he began in each of us (Philippians 1:6). This means that God is doing his transforming work in the person you are caring for and also transforming you as you face the challenges of caregiving. He is perfecting the character of Christ in both of you in the midst of your struggles.

Everyone Has a Body and a Soul

You and the person you are caring for have a body *and* a soul (Genesis 2:7; Ecclesiastes 12:7; John 3:6;

2 Corinthians 4:16–18). The Bible tells us that we consist of two aspects: the spirit (or soul, heart, mind, inner person) and the body (or flesh, outer person).

When we speak of the "spirit" or "heart" we are talking about issues of motivation, belief, being for or against God, righteousness or unrighteousness, emotion, and the will to act. When we speak of the body we are thinking in terms of health versus illness and strengths versus weaknesses. Some of these distinctions are easier than others: Gossip and hatred are clearly issues of the heart. On the other hand, a stroke, Alzheimer's disease, or traumatic brain injury are clearly issues of the body. You can repent of hatred, but you can't repent of Alzheimer's disease.

We need to remember these two aspects of who we are because we are prone to extremes. Either we focus on the physical aspects of our existence and downplay the spiritual aspect of our image bearing, *or* we focus on the spiritual aspects of our personhood and minimize the physical aspects.

Instead, *both* body and heart must be taken into consideration in your caregiving. You must address both bodily weakness and heart-generated sin. What you see on display in the personality of the person you are caring for—the total package of how a person engages God and others at the level of thoughts, emotions, motives, and actions—is a combination of bodily strengths and weaknesses as well as heart motivations.

Some things are weighted toward the body/brain (George's paralysis) and some things are weighted toward the heart (George's angry outbursts and lewd comments), but there is a lot of overlap isn't there? George's passivity *could* come from a love of comfort and ease that leads him to withdraw from his family, rather than engage in the hard work of communicating with them. But physical and mental fatigue is a common aftershock of a stroke, which suggests that physical weakness is present too.

So effective, wise caregiving asks these questions:

- Which behaviors are weighted toward the spiritual (issues of obedience or disobedience)?
- Which behaviors are weighted toward the physical (issues of weakness and suffering)?

• Or is this behavior—as it so often is—a combination of both bodily limitation and spiritual issues?

Asking these questions will clarify and give direction for your caregiving. Not knowing how to understand and process the behaviors you are seeing increases the difficulty of caregiving. Understanding the distinction between the spiritual and physical will help you to know when you should offer comfort and when you should challenge a behavior.

Don't be surprised that people struggle more spiritually after a physical event such as a stroke or in the context of a chronic illness, given the tight connection between the body and heart. Bodily weakness impacts us spiritually. The physical affects the spiritual for better or for worse. But you can remind the person you are caring for that Jesus continues his inward renewal in our lives even as our bodies weaken (2 Corinthians 4:16).

Encourage the person you are caring for to ask the Spirit for daily help. Although unique temptations are attached to his or her disability, the apostle Paul reminds us, "No temptation has seized you except what is common to man. And God is faithful; he will not let you be tempted beyond what you can bear. But when you are tempted, he will also provide a way out so that you can stand up under it" (1 Corinthians 10:13). Every day remind the person you are caring for of God's faithfulness, and pray together for the grace to endure.

Be Aware of Your Temptations

Just as the person you are caring for has unique temptations, so you, as a caregiver, will also be tempted in certain areas. Let me mention three common struggles: anger, fear, and indispensability.

Are you struggling with anger? How can you tell if you are struggling with anger toward God or toward the person you are caring for? Ask yourself if you have any of these thoughts:

- I want relief and God is not delivering.
- Can't anything go smoothly? All I wanted was....

- I deserve better than this.
- All I want is to be a normal family.
- God has put more on my plate than I can deal with.

Are you struggling with fear? Your fears and anxieties often express themselves in thoughts like these:

- What if things get worse? I know I couldn't handle that!
- There's no way I can do this for the long haul.
- I see nothing but heartache for the rest of our lives.
- Unless I minister rightly, I'll make the situation worse.
- How will we ever pay for all the medical bills?

Do you think you are indispensable? If your whole life is so wrapped up in caregiving that you ignore other relationships, even your own physical and spiritual life, then you may be struggling with the "indispensability syndrome." This syndrome sounds like this:

- Nobody can do it better than I can.
- Nobody cares except for me.
- If I don't do it, nobody will.

When you see these three things (and more!) in your heart, turn to the Lord and find his grace, mercy, and help in your time of need (Hebrews 4:16). Against anger, meditate on the fact that God who did not spare his own Son, the most lavish gift of all, will not withhold from us what we really need (Romans 8:32). Against fear, hear Jesus say, "Do not be afraid, little flock, for your Father has been pleased to give you the kingdom" (Luke 12:32). Against a sense of indispensability and self-sufficiency, remember that God's strength is actually "made perfect in weakness" (2 Corinthians 12:9).

Remember, you and the person you are caring for are more alike than you are different. You are both made in the image of God. God wants to transform both of you so you will be a beautiful reflection of his image to the watching world. This transformation happens as you ask God every day for wisdom and power through his Spirit, and by faith depend on him for everything you need for life and godliness (2 Peter 1:3).

Watch for Signs of "Caregiver Burnout"

When caregivers experience "burnout," that means they have run out of the spiritual, physical, and social resources that fuel the engine of their daily lives. So what are the warning signs that your gas tank is getting empty? Let me categorize these signs in social, physical, and spiritual terms.

Social warning signs:

- You have little or no time for relationships outside the home.
- You and your spouse spend little time talking.
- Your involvement with your children has significantly decreased.
- There are ongoing, unresolved tensions between you and your spouse or between you and your children.

- You feel like there is no one to talk with who can understand your struggles.
- You feel isolated and alone.
- Your job performance is declining.

Physical warning signs:

- Your sleep is regularly interrupted.
- You feel tired and physically run down most of the time.
- You have stopped exercising.
- You are overeating or under-eating.
- You have frequent headaches or indigestion.
- You have difficulty concentrating or making decisions.
- You have other new health problems.

Spiritual warning signs: (I am including your emotional and thought life in this category because the Bible assumes our emotions, thoughts, and actions flow, first and foremost, out of our relationship to God.)

- You have stopped reading the Bible and praying.

- You have withdrawn from church life.
- You feel like nobody cares about you.
- You resent the amount of time that you spend caregiving.
- You have little or no joy in life.
- You feel depressed or hopeless.
- You feel like you are just "going through the motions."
- You are having crying spells.
- You feel anxious and overwhelmed much of the time.
- You act edgy and irritable much of the time.
- You consistently don't sense God's presence and power equipping you for the ministry tasks at hand.

You need to guard against becoming a perpetual caregiving machine, both physically and mentally. No doubt, as you have found, there *is* a need to be more proactive, more thoughtful, and more sacrificial than you ever anticipated. Although it's a cliché, it's true: When it comes to ministry, you can't give what you haven't got. If you want to give Christ's grace to your loved one, then you must be experiencing his grace and mercy yourself in your time of need (Hebrews 4:15–16). So don't ignore these warning signs in your life, let them drive you to a deeper dependence on Jesus. You will learn that dependence as you take the following practical steps.

Practical Strategies for Change

Get Ready, Get Set, Be Still!

Unless you practice being still before God, you will forget who God is and that he is your "refuge and strength, an ever-present help in trouble" (Psalm 46:1, 10). So in the midst of the pressures of your life, you need to make sure you don't give up simply sitting at Jesus' feet and learning from him. But because of how much time you spend caregiving, you might need to change your expectations for communing with God. I used to think I couldn't meet with God without a forty-five minute (or more) daily "quiet time," during which I secluded myself for Bible reading and prayer. I still believe that individual prayer and Bible study are important disciplines, but there are many other ways to cultivate your relationship with the Lord. Getting a chunk of time to study the Bible and pray doesn't guarantee that it will be a fruitful time! I have had many quiet times that were so quiet I fell asleep! You might need to scale down your expectations for times of individual study and prayer—perhaps having several ten-minute blocks of time would be more feasible than one longer time.

Beyond your devotional times, consider how to "practice the presence of God" (Brother Lawrence's phrase) in the midst of day-to-day activities. Here are some ideas:

- *Live out of ongoing dependent prayer.* Realize and voice (whether out loud or silently) in the midst of any activity that God by his Spirit is with you. Call out to him in the midst of difficulty. Talk to him as you do menial activities like cleaning the kitchen or changing the sheets on the bed. While you may find it challenging to set aside time for prayer, I believe this "prayer on the fly" builds into your life an ongoing dependence on God's grace. Prayer then becomes a lifestyle, not simply an event.

- *Cultivate thankfulness.* Often our relationship with God weakens when we lose sight of his provision for our lives. Proactively determine to thank and praise him for the many ways each day he cares for you, the caregiver. Ask him to give you eyes to see the small blessings he sends your way (Romans 8:32).
- *If possible, involve the person you are caring for.* The extent to which you can do this depends on the person you are caring for. But you can try reading out loud short passages from the Bible, singing hymns (even if you don't have a good voice!), and praying (even if you are the only one who can speak).
- *Listen to worship music or sermons while you are caregiving.* This might initially feel unfocused, but you will be surprised by how much you will benefit by having good music and good teaching in the background.

Communion with God also occurs when his people gather for worship, especially when partaking of the Lord's Supper. Make sure that you have enough help so that you can regularly meet with God's people (Hebrews 10:25).

Attend to Your Own Health

Don't forget that Jesus, in the whirlwind of ministry, ate, drank, slept, and hung out with sinners and saints alike. Ongoing physical fatigue, sleeplessness, or postponement of your own health-related issues will ultimately undermine your ability to minister wisely and compassionately. So make sure you are attending to your own health, even in the midst of caring for the needs of another person.

Plow Your Own Heart

The concentration camp survivor Victor Frankl said, "When we are no longer able to change a situation, we are challenged to change ourselves." You may not be able to change the chronic, life-altering aspects of your loved one's physical or mental struggle, but you can be sure that God is intent on transforming you more fully into the character of Christ as you care for your loved one.

Plow your own heart by evaluating how your desires, demands, fears, insecurities, wants, and expectations are impacting your ability to give care. Look back at the section about your temptations. Ask God to show you the areas in your life where you are struggling. Where do your "if onlys" lead? Asking these questions will reveal what you treasure the most and what can replace your submission to God's wise design for your life.

Be an Instrument of Redemption

Ask God to give you the wisdom to know what you *are responsible* for dealing with and what you *are not responsible* for dealing with. You are called to be your brother's keeper, not your brother's savior! In every situation, there are some things God calls us to do, that we can't pass on to anyone else. These are our responsibilities, and God promises the resources to faithfully obey his calling at that moment. But there are many things that *concern* us and yet are beyond our abilities to control or to bring change.[1]

Consider George. What are some of the specific

responsibilities God is calling George's family to? They are called to pray for George. They are called to live out what Paul says in Ephesians 4:31–32: "Get rid of all bitterness, rage and anger, brawling and slander, along with every form of malice. Be kind and compassionate to one another, forgiving each other, just as in Christ God forgave you."

That means not responding in kind when George attacks in anger; it means practicing forbearance and forgiveness when George sins against them. But in addition, they are called to bring the truth of the gospel into George's life, seeking to restore him gently (Galatians 6:1). They are called to enter George's world and to understand as much as they can about the "whys" of his particular struggles, and then incarnate the love the Christ to him.

What should George's family be concerned about, but not view as *their* ultimate responsibility? Well, certainly, George's responses! They are not responsible for how George responds, even though it may be heart-wrenching to them. As much as George's family might desire him to change, and as much as God might call them to create a context that may help George to change (going back to what I said about responsibility), their mission cannot be to "fix" George. Only God can bring that kind of change. Should they be concerned that George increasingly honor Christ by the way he interacts with others? Yes! Should they be concerned that he repents when he sins? Yes! But for these things they must entrust George to God. Having this atti- tude of prayerful trust will help to clarify when more specific action (responsibility) is needed.

Sometimes you will err on the side of watching and waiting when you should be taking corrective, restor- ative action with your loved one. And other times you will err on the side of taking too much responsibility in the care of your family member. Thank the Lord when he shows you that choosing a different path would have been helpful. But then move forward, praying for his promised wisdom to guide you in the midst of your ongoing challenges (James 1:2–5).

When you believe you are called to act (and not simply pray and wait), tailor your approach to the person you are caring for based on the body-spirit distinctions we already discussed. Recognize the limitations that the body/brain places upon your family member and respond accordingly. Your expectations for the other person will vary based on the physical strengths and weaknesses he has.

Live in Community

In the Bible, depending on others is the normal way to live. Please don't suffer in silence; instead ask for help. Ask family, friends, and your church community to help you. And then accept the help that is offered. Even if those who help might not do things exactly like you, they can still be a blessing to you. Combat your tendency to be "the indispensable one" by sharing your struggles with those around you and accepting the support that others give.

Providing holistic care to someone whose chronic illness you cannot fix is both difficult and redemptive at the same time. Let Paul's words encourage you today: "Therefore, my dear brothers, stand firm. Let nothing move you. Always give yourselves fully to the work of the Lord, because you know that your labor in the Lord is not in vain" (1 Corinthians 15:58). God has entrusted you with a unique opportunity to minister the gospel of Jesus Christ in both word and deed. Although you may sometime feel that no one knows what you are going through, God sees you. He knows all about your struggles and sacrifices and he is with you, ready to help you in your time of need.

Endnotes

1. See Paul David Tripp, *Instruments in the Redeemer's Hands,* (Phillipsburg, NJ: P&R, 2002), 250-257.